Everything You Need to Know About Music Lessons

Publisher: Rogers School of Music

Cover Design: Chris & Jen Hickle

Printed by CreateSpace, an Amazon.com company

© 2014 by Brannon Hungness and Jennifer L. Hickle

All rights reserved.

No part of this book may be used or reproduced without written consent by the author.

ISBN: 978-1517512415

www.RogersSchoolofMusic.com

Photos provided by Rogers School of Music

Everything You Need to Know About Music Lessons

A fun and super simple guide about music lessons for you or your children

by

Jen Hickle

About the Author

Jen Hickle graduated from North Central University in 2000 as music graduate of the year. Together with her husband Chris, they own Rogers School of Music, which has earned a number of awards and accolades since its opening in 1998.

Jen has spoken to music majors at Bethel University in St. Paul, North Central University in Minneapolis, and to music studio owners all over the country.

In 2012, Rogers School of Music won a national award for music academy excellence and business growth. This gained the attention of the city of Rogers and she was awarded the Small-Medium Business Excellence Award in 2013. Readers of local papers acknowledged the school's notability by voting Rogers School of Music "Best Music School" for four different newspapers in 2015.

Introduction	**9**
Chapter 1 10 benefits of Learning to Play a Musical Instrument	**17**
Chapter 2 Choosing an Instrument	**31**
Chapter 3 10 Things to Look for in a Music Lessons Provider	**49**
Chapter 4 Benefits of Music Lessons for Children	**63**
Chapter 5 Benefits of Music Lessons for Teens	**67**
Chapter 6 Benefits of Music Lessons for Adults	**70**
Chapter 7 Benefits of Music Lessons for the Whole Family	**73**
Chapter 8 10 Practicing Tips	**77**
Chapter 9 Online Learning as a Great Supplement	**101**
Chapter 10 Finding Your Place in Music	**105**

Introduction

I believe that everyone can connect with music. Music can change your mood, lift your spirit, bring memories flooding back, or set the mood for any occasion.

Music can help you focus, calm you down, or add suspense and intrigue to your favorite movie. Music is all around you and in all you do!

When I was in school, music was my favorite class. I loved to sing and I loved to play the piano. I competed in singing and piano competitions, and was selected to perform in talent shows and participate in select choirs and ensembles. In high school, I continued to sing and also played flute and percussion in the school band. I loved to sing in the choir and also accompany on the piano. My free time was often spent learning about new recording artists, buying music, and attending concerts.

My love of music grew as I entered college and learned about songwriting, worship leading, and choral directing.

I come from a long line of musicians and I love hearing stories from my aunts and grandparents about their love for music. Hearing our entire family sing together is a wonderful joy!

Now that I'm a mom, I understand another side of music, too. I love helping my own kids find their passion for music through piano, voice, violin, guitar, bass, theatre, and more. They have all tried various instruments and I love seeing their knowledge and excitement for music grow!

When I was growing up, my mom was a music teacher, but I never imagined that I would follow in her footsteps. I started teaching piano to a few neighbor kids when I was only 18 years old, and I quickly learned that I loved it! I taught piano lessons all throughout college (and was mentored by my college professors) and graduated debt-free because of my little side business!

My mission was clear-- it didn't matter if my students were taking lessons just for fun, for just one year, or if they would eventually have music as their career. (I'm proud to tell you that one of my first piano students is getting her master's degree in piano right now!) I determined that I would give them all the best music education possible. Within only a couple years, I was teaching 20 students a week, and had even acquired a waiting list. So I started hiring piano teachers for my new company: Signature School of Music (later renamed Rogers School of Music). I was determined to hire only the very best teachers so they could mentor students in the very best way! In doing so, I could expand my influence and impact even more children and adults. Within just a few short years, my little company had 100 students taking lessons with outstanding teachers, who were passionate about excellence. However, I quickly got overwhelmed—I was managing many teachers, students, book orders and the billing—and I was busy with 4 little babies at home, too! Out of necessity, I intentionally began down-sizing and threw myself into learning about business and marketing so I could grow my company the right way.

Today, Rogers School of Music has 400+ students, over 25 teachers, and a location in Rogers, MN. I homeschool my four kids, and my research about education has only further fueled my passion for music lessons. The more I learn about learning styles, personalities, learning challenges, and education methods, the more passionate I become!

This little book is a handbook for you to learn everything you need to know about music lessons! Maybe you don't have a mom or aunt or grandma that is a music teacher, and you don't know where to start. There is a wealth of information online that can be quite overwhelming and confusing!

To help you along your journey, I've intentionally put all the most commonly asked questions in one place, so you, too, can be confident about your decisions as you journey down the wonderful path of music education for yourself or your child!

Passionate about music education,

Jen Hickle
Rogers, MN

Everything You Need to Know About Music Lessons

This book is dedicated to future musicians everywhere.

Chapter 1

10 Benefits of Learning to Play a Musical Instrument

Wow! Did you know that playing a musical instrument can change the structure of your brain?

This may sound like something out of a sci-fi movie, but it is actually a medically proven phenomenon! And even better, these particular brain changes offer many positive benefits.

So let's choose 10 benefits and look at them in detail. There are many more, but these are some of the most important.

1. Our thought processes are improved.

Musically trained people typically outperform non-musically trained people on cognitive tasks.

They perform better on tests of word recall, nonverbal memory, and cognitive flexibility.

Other results show that playing an instrument can increase your IQ by as many as seven points.

2. Our time management and organizational skills become improved.

Music, by nature, is timed. So in order to learn to play, students must learn to organize their thoughts in terms of time structures.

For instance, when learning a new piece, a student will begin to dissect the composition, focusing on the difficult passages first. This strategy is extremely efficient, and allows the student to progress more quickly as a musician.

When the student sees the resulting improvement, it creates even more motivation!

Therefore, music students will gradually train their brains to process *all* new information in terms of time and structure. This aids in the management and organization of tasks, extending far beyond the playing of their instruments.

3. Our coordination becomes enhanced

The sections of your brain that control motor skills actually grow larger and become more active when you learn to play a musical instrument.

In order to create music that sounds like music, your brain must translate thoughts and notations into specific motor patterns. As a result, your brain learns to master fingerings, rhythm, and even breathing, all at once!

Plus, for most instruments, you need to be able to have your fingers, arms, and sometimes even your legs each performing different tasks at the same time. This enhanced coordination can aid students in sports, typing, dancing, and much more!

4. Music relieves stress

Playing music, or even just listening to it, is a great way to relieve stress.

It doesn't matter if the music is soothing or extremely exciting--either will help you get lost in the sea of sound. And when you are totally immersed, it's much easier to relax!

Playing an instrument also releases endorphins into your body, which naturally reduces your stress level.

5. Our memory capacity and empathy increases.

Playing a musical instrument helps the mind to be alert and remain active, eventually improving the memory.

Learning a foreign language, for instance, will become easier. Musicians also tend to be more accurate in interpreting other people's emotions.

Playing an instrument requires you to recognize sounds and tones. This increases your ability to store audio information, allowing for more proficiency in your own language, too.

6. Our aptitude for math skyrockets

Playing music requires the counting of notes and rhythms. This helps to reinforce and improve math skills.

The concepts and ideas involved with music theory are heavily influenced by mathematical concepts.

Students of music have a much easier time understanding concepts about fractions, percentages, and even geometry, because they already have experience with similar thought patterns.

7. Our confidence and self-expression become ignited!

When you reach a certain point in your musical education, you'll be able to express yourself by playing whatever kind of music you want.

You might even write your own music, and it could be in a whole new style that no one has even heard yet!

Music can become a great outlet for your emotions.

Playing a musical instrument builds self-esteem and a strong sense of identity.

8. Playing music provides health benefits.

Playing music has many soothing effects on the mind and body.

Studies suggest that music therapy helps children and teens with attention deficit hyperactivity disorder (ADHD), insomnia, and depression. Playing music has been found to reduce blood pressure levels in musicians of all ages.

Also, drumming, or rocking out some wild moves on another instrument, can burn as many as 500 calories during one session.

9. Music lessons teach discipline, responsibility and perseverance.

It takes effort to learn how to play a musical instrument. And when you start getting good at your new skill, you get to see just how much that effort has paid off.

It's ultimately up to the student to put in the work. Once you get to a certain level, you will realize that with dedication, the sky is the limit!

Maintaining a consistent practice schedule is important, as it trains the student to be disciplined. The lessons and skills learned from consistent practice builds commitment, and aids in many other aspects of life.

10. It's just plain fun!

Playing music is a blast!

There's nothing better than getting totally engrossed in the song blasting through your headphones, or raucously rocking out with friends or bandmates.

Even when you're just getting started, playing some basic songs is super fun! No matter how simple, there's nothing better than being able to say "I just made music!"

Chapter 2

Choosing an Instrument

If you or your child have not yet chosen an instrument to play, I have a few pieces of advice for you to consider.

First off, desire is important! It should be an instrument you love hearing and really **want** to play.

But don't feel pressured. It's okay if you change your mind later. Some students start with an instrument and eventually switch to a different one. Just as students change and grow, so do their tastes and interests. The great thing is that a lot of what you learn on one instrument is directly transferrable to other instruments.

Let's take a look at a few things to consider with five of the most popular instruments.

Voice:

In a way, you're already set to go for vocal lessons. After all, you don't need to go out and buy a voice!

You can learn any style of music you like, and your teacher, after having a lesson or two to get acquainted with your preferences, can recommend what music or books will work best for you.

Also, you'll want to find backing tracks of the songs you'd like to sing. These are readily available on sites like YouTube.

Even though you don't have to hit keys or pluck strings when you sing, the voice is still a specific instrument, even though it is internal. Warm-ups and breathing techniques are fundamental to properly using your voice. Visualization and acting techniques will help you to learn how to express yourself when singing.

I also recommend that singers learn to play guitar or piano. This way, they can provide their own accompaniment. Plus, it will help you gain even more knowledge about music in general. Even just learning the basics will significantly increase the range of what you can do with your voice and your music.

Piano:

Many people are concerned that they will need a piano at home in order to take piano lessons. This is not the case! It is perfectly fine to start out on an inexpensive keyboard. For the first few years of learning, you will be familiarizing yourself with the notes up and down the keyboard. Generally speaking, the order and sounds of the keys remains the same, regardless of the brand or cost.

Some keyboards have weighted keys and feel very much like playing a real piano. The best part of a keyboard is being able to use headphones and make music in your own little world! Plus, you can often record and play back what you are learning, which is very fun!

When you are ready, I highly recommend these 3 things when buying a keyboard: 88 keys, weighted keys, and a pedal. This will make your experience enjoyable and less frustrating!

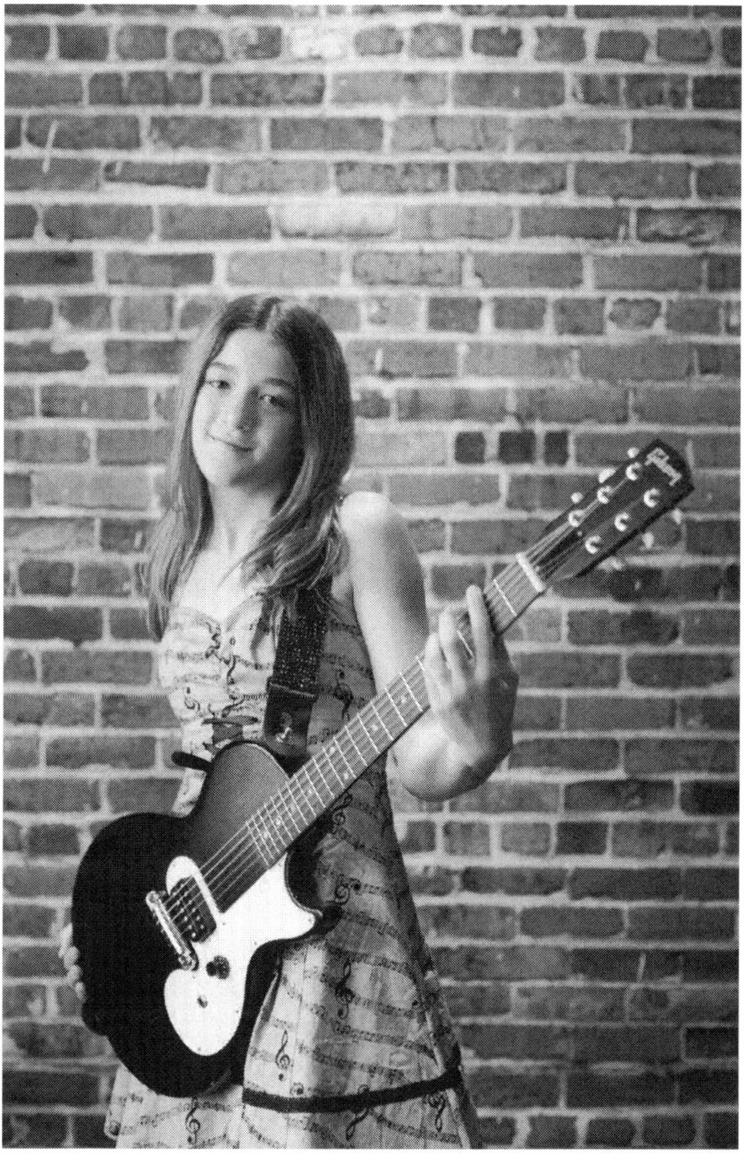

Guitar:

When starting lessons, the most important thing is to pick the right guitar. If you don't have the right kind of guitar, pressing the strings down can be hard and painful. Beginners can start on an electric or a nylon string acoustic guitar—this will eliminate the pain and make playing more fun at the start of lessons!

There are electric guitars and acoustic guitars. Acoustic guitars are either steel string or nylon string.

There are many high-quality, easy to play guitars that are very affordable. It just takes a little time to find the right ones-- an effort that will certainly pay off once you start to play.

Still, even with an easy-to-play guitar, there is a period during the first few weeks where your fingertips will get a little sore. This is normal! Don't feel discouraged. Your fingers will toughen up shortly, and pressing the strings will begin to feel as natural to you as any daily activity.

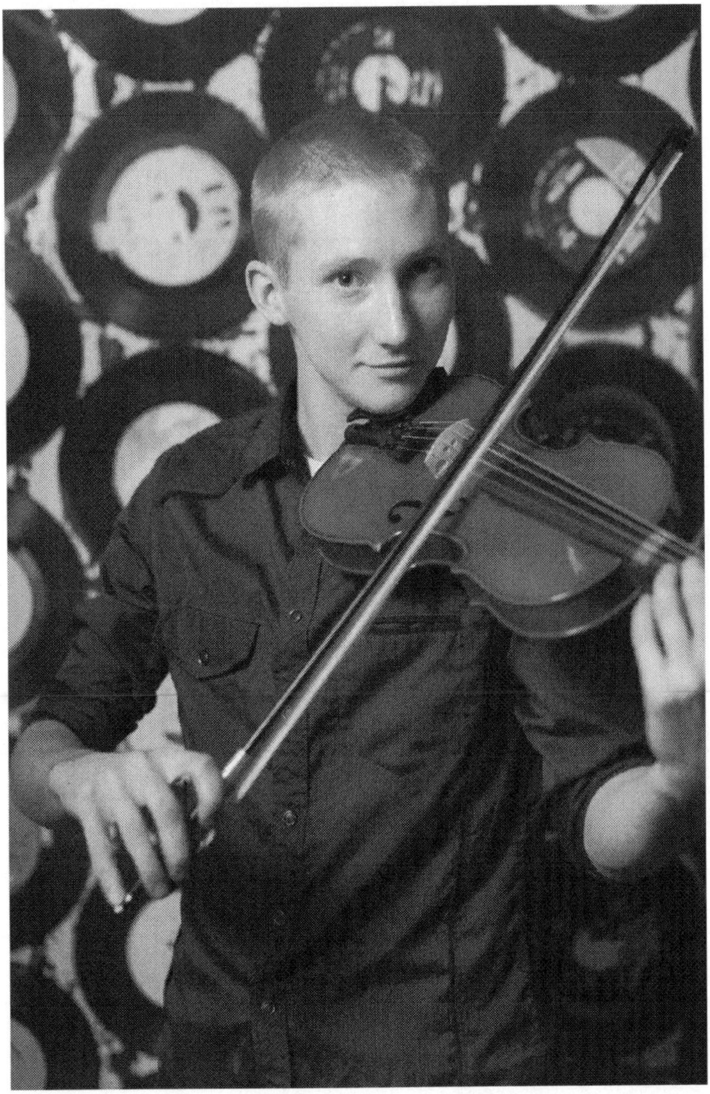

Violin:

First off, it's extremely important to have a violin that's the right size for you. If you are an adult, a full size (4/4) violin will be a good fit. For the younger student, a smaller instrument will most likely be more appropriate.

The best way to ensure that you have the proper size is to visit a store that specializes in stringed instruments. The professionals there will be able to measure you, and determine the size of violin that will best fit your body.

Beware of cheap violins in mail-order catalogues, online, or in stores that do not specialize in stringed instruments. Some of these are practically toys, and can be pretty much unplayable!

New violinists will learn to coordinate the fingering and the bowing of their instrument. And the lack of frets on the violin creates an additional challenge. As a result, a beginner violinist doesn't generally produce the most pleasant tones right away. So don't be dismayed if you or the student in your home sounds a bit squawky at first. This is all part of the process, and the tone will improve greatly over time.

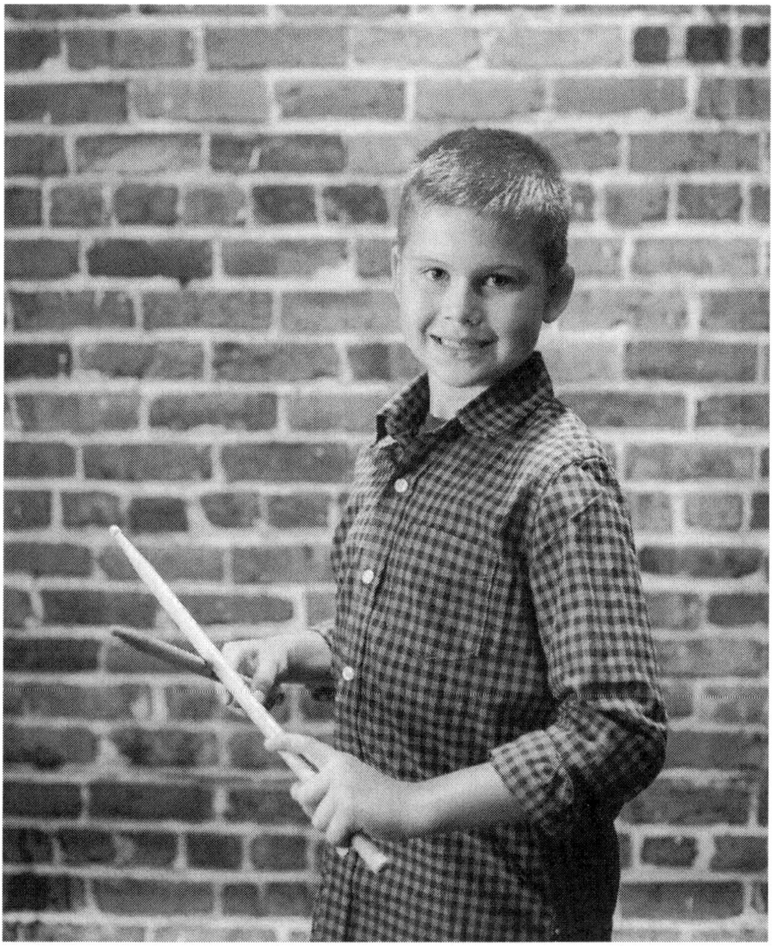

Drums:

There are a few things to consider about starting drum lessons.

Most students want to start off playing the kit. If that's where the desire is, that's the direction to take. Do what makes the student happy!

However, it is also fine, and very common, to start off with some sticks and a practice pad. This is an inexpensive way to start learning some basic rhythms. If you choose to go this direction, I would recommend getting a kit within 3 to 4 months after starting. It's just a whole lot more exciting, and will keep the student's interest strong!

By nature, drums are loud! To preserve the ears, I recommend using shooting range ear muffs or earplugs when playing for a long period of time. You can also practice by running a backing track through headphones!

Electronic drums are also an option. Depending on your living situation (and your desire to preserve a relationship with your neighbors!) it's nice to be able to turn the volume up or down.

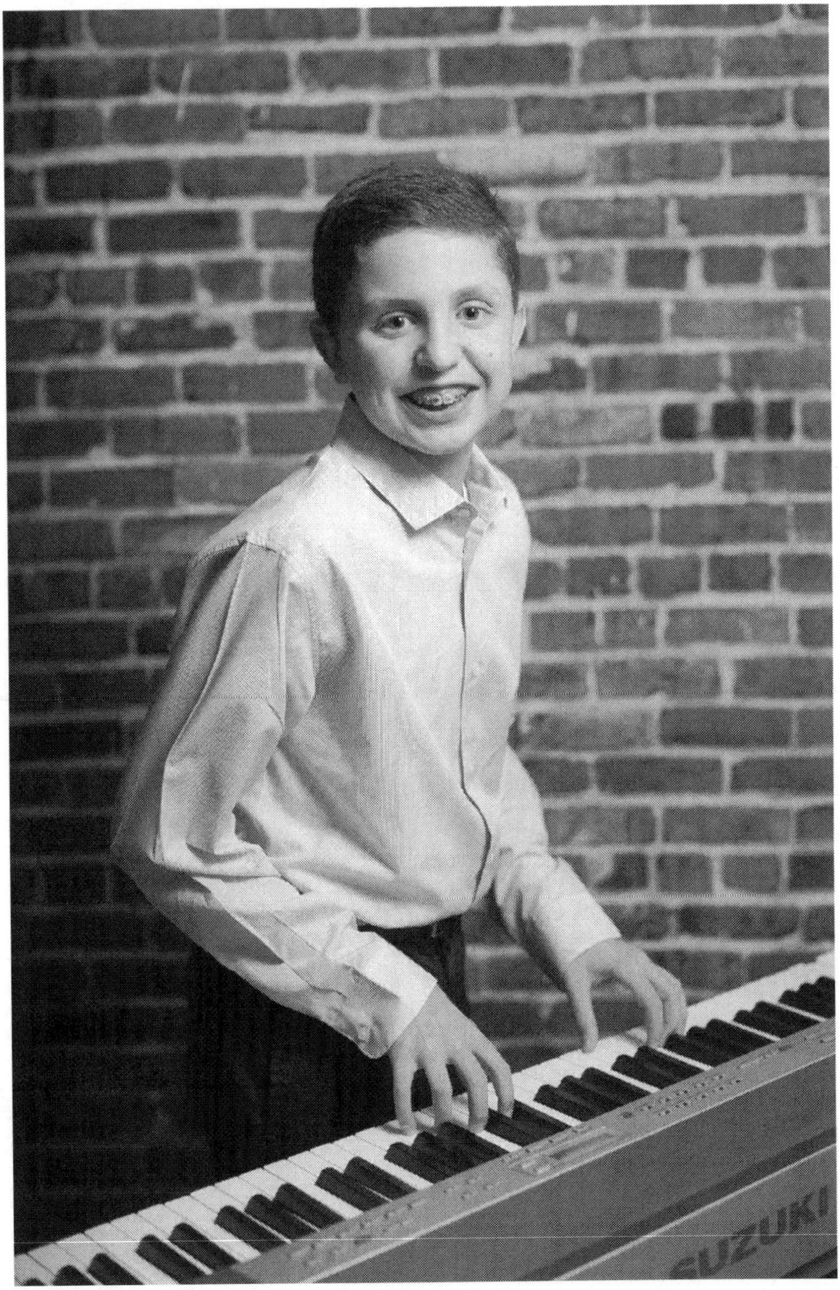
SUZUKI

Chapter 3

10 Things to Look for in a Music Lessons Provider

Not all music lessons are the same. It's important to find a lessons provider that will fulfill your needs as an individual. Here are some guidelines that I recommend:

1. Take lessons with a teacher who is fun.

Having a teacher who has a fun, positive attitude makes learning easier. You will feel inspired and encouraged-- like you can take on the world!

2. Take lessons at a school designed for private lessons.

Lessons in your home or lessons at a teacher's house are riddled with distractions. Phone calls, texting, household tasks, cooking smells, and other disruptions can lead to non-productive lesson time. Plus, many students end up feeling *too* comfortable at home, which can lead to a more lax attitude during lessons.

Often, teachers involved in these kinds of lessons lack structure in their lesson plans.

A school designed for private lessons should have office staff who takes care of all the scheduling, so the teacher is free to focus all of their attention on you. When teachers are distracted by things like scheduling and client phone calls, it can be difficult for them to focus on their priorities. A teacher's #1 priority should always be to give you the best lesson experience possible.

3. Take lessons at a school run by a music lessons authority.

There are many factors involved with teaching private music lessons. When a school is run by not just a businessperson or musician, but someone who has many years of teaching experience, they know specifically what to look for in teachers they hire at their school.

4. Take lessons at a school that has multiple teachers for each instrument.

Music teachers come and go. Like all of us, they sometimes have to move or experience unavoidable family commitments. I changed piano teachers many times when I was young and my mom was constantly on the lookout for my next teacher. We constantly had to start the whole process over again to find another good teacher. When you take lessons at a school with multiple teachers, changing teachers becomes easy. These teachers were all hired by the same music lessons authority and thus have similar teaching styles and standards.

5. Take lessons with a teacher who will teach you the music you want to play.

This seems like a given, but actually, many teachers insist on teaching in the same style in which they were taught. These teachers don't pay attention to what their students are interested in, because they are hung-up on one particular teaching method. You will want to start with a teacher who is extremely versatile and can show you how to play not only by the book, but also by ear. The best teachers also utilize available technology, like laptops and tablets.

6. Take lessons at a place with a pleasant atmosphere and a community of like-minded students.

When you see others around you taking lessons and having fun, it inspires you to stick with it and become truly amazing!

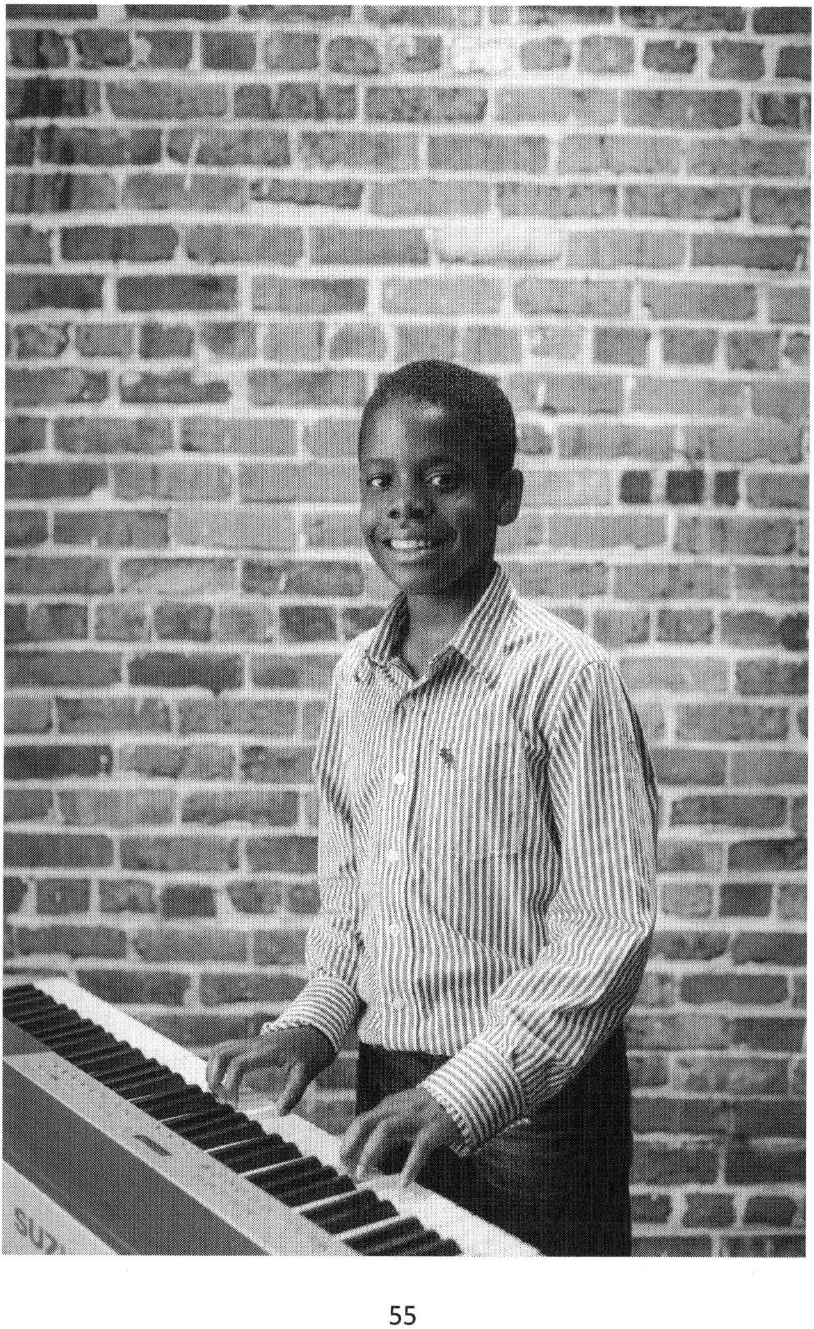

7. Take lessons from a provider who offers at least two recitals a year.

Every student deserves the opportunity to perform in recitals. After all, it's your chance to show off all that talent and hard work!

Many students feel nervous before their first recital. Nervousness is normal, and can even be seen as a positive—it shows that you care about what you are doing! The truth is, you will gain so much confidence after having performed. Recitals can really help students move forward, as they are a great way to set concrete goals. Also, it's fun and inspiring to see what the other students do!

Despite the benefits, recitals should never be mandatory. Students should choose to participate when they are ready. Sometimes it builds confidence to just come and watch.

8. Take lessons at a school that hosts community events throughout the year.

Events like these are important, because they help a student build relationships. Often, you will get the chance to hear your teacher perform, and you are likely to meet fellow students who have similar interests to yours. When you become an active part of something larger, you no longer feel like you're doing it on your own. You will have a new support system. Getting more involved creates enthusiasm, because it's simply much more exciting!

9. Take lessons at a place that clients rave about.

Does your lessons provider have testimonials on their website? And what do they say? When you find a place where the clients' words really resonate with you, that's where you should go.

10. Did I mention that you should take lessons from somewhere that's fun?

I know I did, but I want to stress it one more time! Students who enjoy their lessons do so much better and progress so much faster.

Lessons should have structure.
Lessons should be informative.
Lessons should be inspiring. And…

Music lessons should be fun!

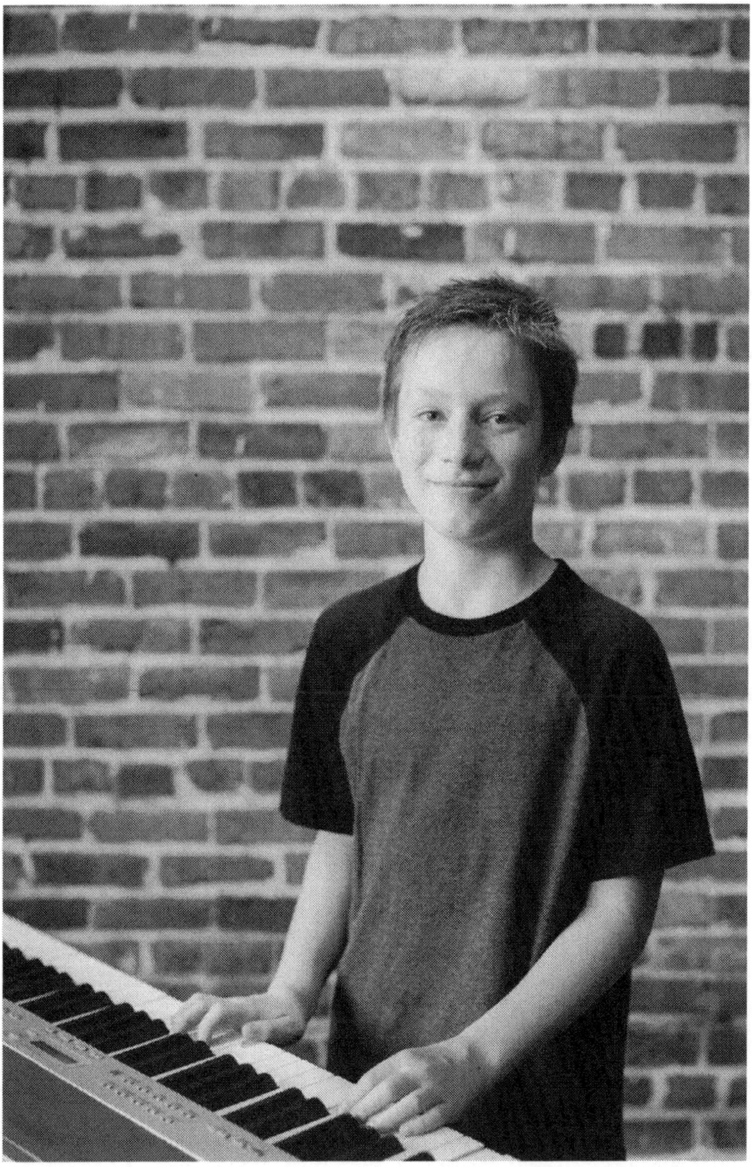

Benefits of taking music lessons for people of different ages

Lessons aren't just for one age group! Next, I will address some benefits that students of different ages will be privy to by taking music lessons. Again, these are by no means the only benefits, just some of the most noteworthy.

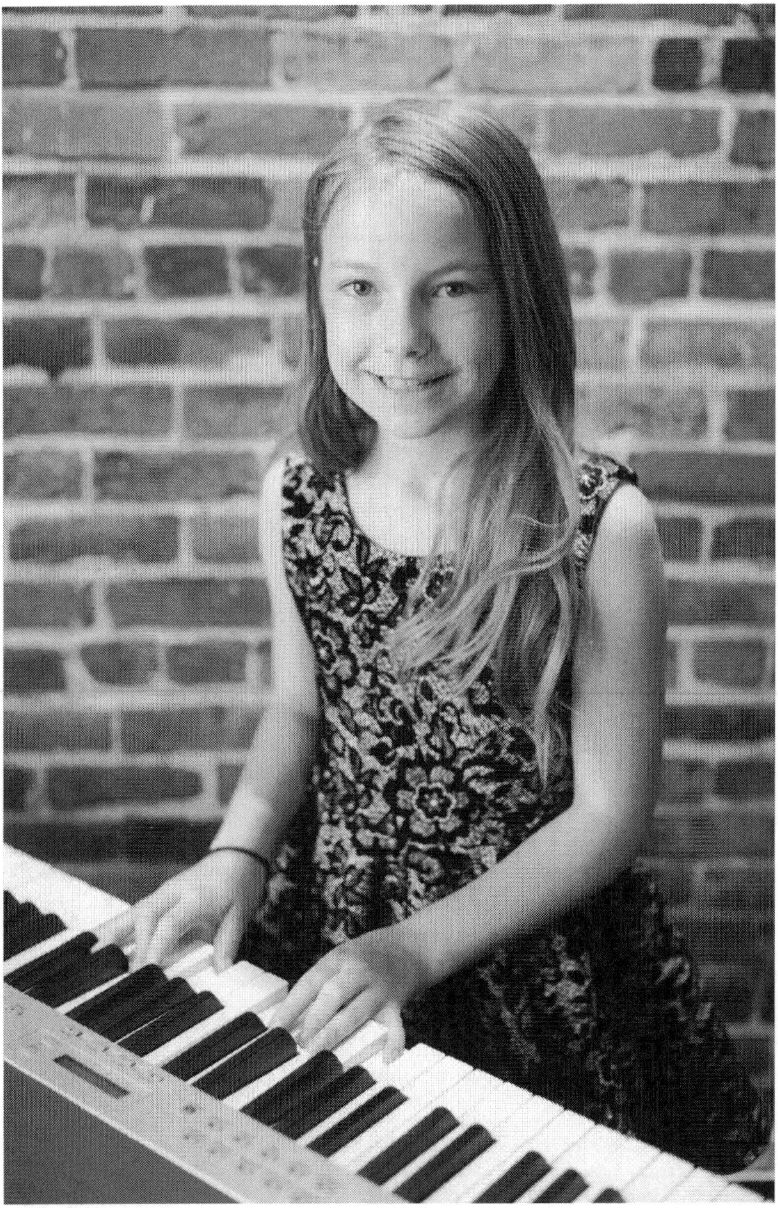

Chapter 4

Benefits of Music Lessons for Children

1. Children who take music lessons often have larger vocabularies and better reading skills than children who do not take lessons.

2. Children who take music lessons are more likely to excel in various forms of study, work more effectively in teams, exhibit better critical thinking skills, stay enrolled in school, graduate, and pursue higher education.

3. Recent studies have shown that children who start and continue with music lessons statistically have lower reports of substance

abuse (tobacco, alcohol, and illicit drugs).

4. Children who play music typically spend less time watching TV.

5. Children who play music display higher self-esteem and are more optimistic.

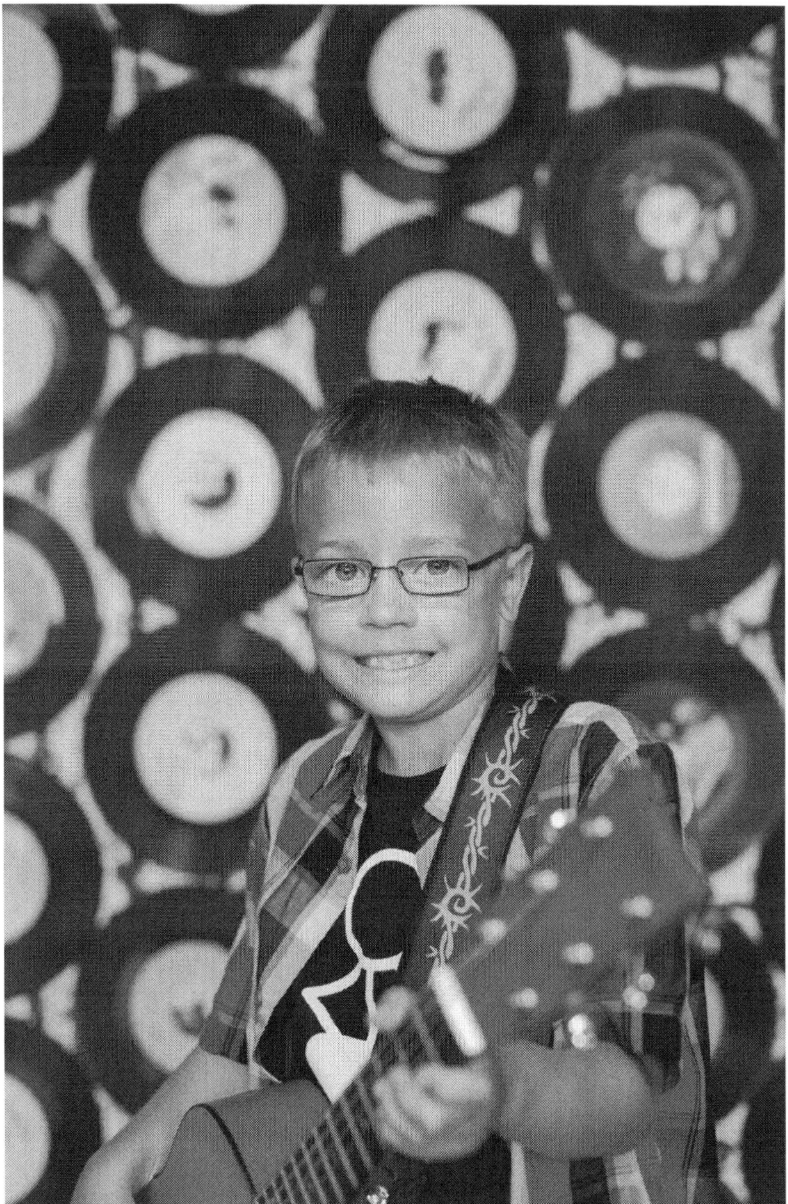

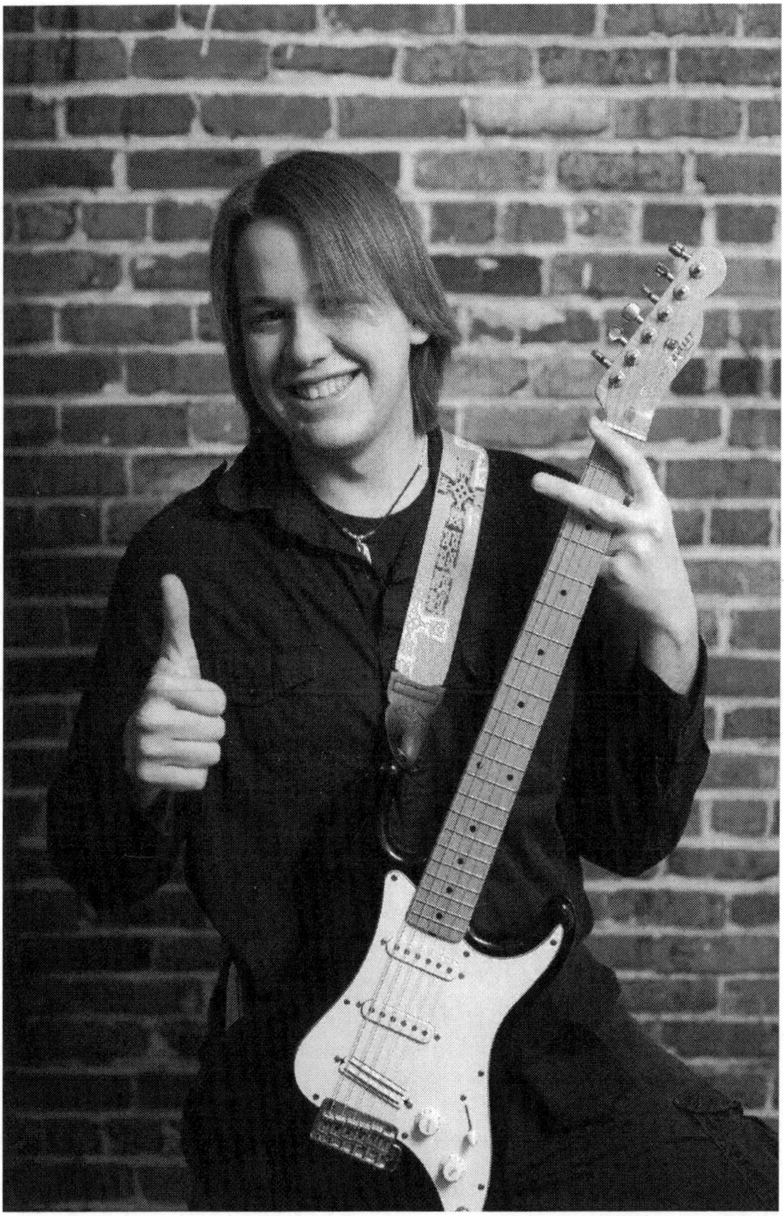

Chapter 5

Benefits of Music Lessons for Teens

1. Students who start taking music lessons during their teen or childhood years score higher on SATs, ACTs, and other tests.

2. Teens who play music form closer social bonds with other like-minded teens.

3. Teens who study music are typically more apt at expressing themselves and their ideas to teachers, parents, and their peers.

4. Studies have shown that teens who study music are not only more creative, but statistically more open-minded and accepting

of different cultures, and ways of thinking.

5. Mastery in music and arts is closely correlated to higher earnings in the future.

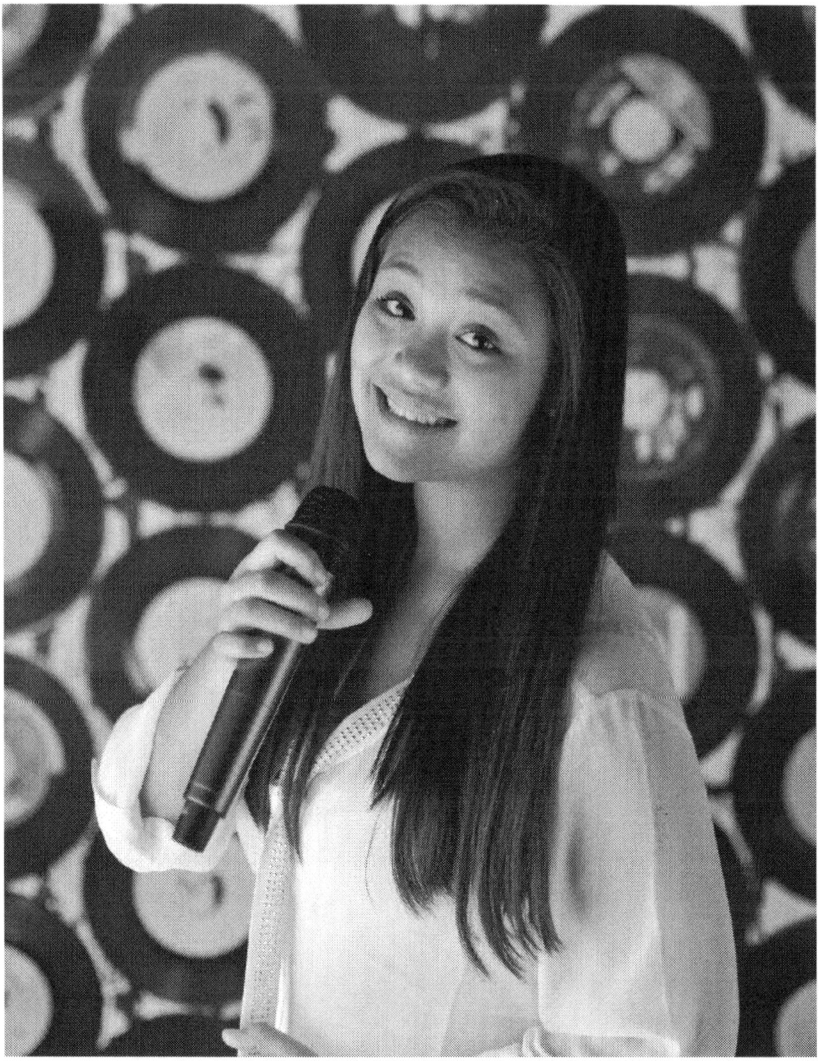

Chapter 6

Benefits of Music Lessons for Adults

1. Adults who play music are typically more focused at work. Communication with their coworkers, family, and friends becomes more effective.

2. Playing music helps to release tension and reduce stress.

3. Playing music is a great way to have fun with friends and meet new people with similar interests.

4. Music lessons help adults stay mentally focused, active, and vibrant.

5. 82% of adults say they wish they had learned to play a musical instrument as a child. It's not too late! Some of my best students have been adults, including seniors in their 70s and 80s.

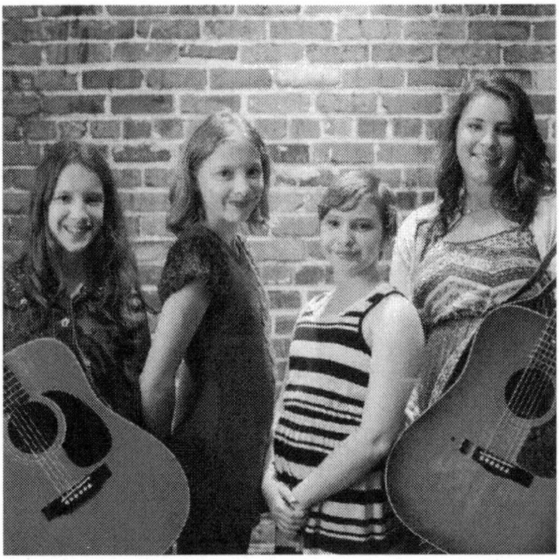

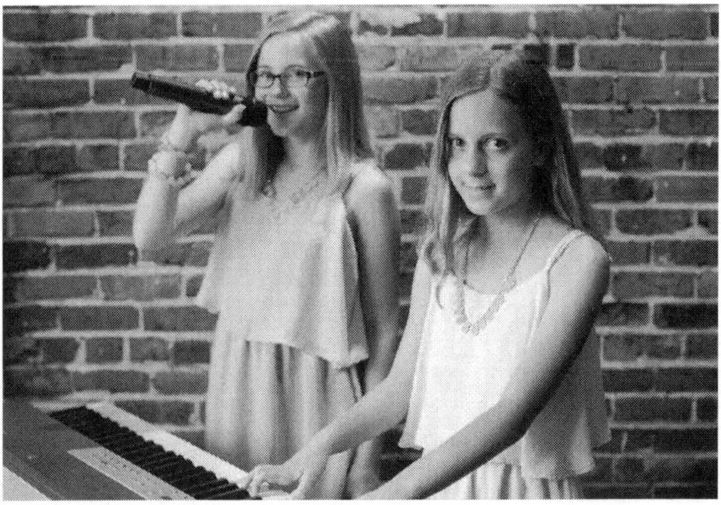

Chapter 7

Benefits of Music Lessons for the Whole Family

Quite often, when a child or teen student begins taking music lessons, a sibling or parent will start taking lessons as well. Although such family support is not necessary to become a wonderful musician on your own, it's still a great idea!

Here are some of the benefits.

1. It's easier to maintain a practice schedule when there's more than one person participating. It's practice time, and the whole family knows it!

2. Healthy competition can push multiple family members to strive for their best.

3. Family members with advanced abilities can help the others out. Teaching family members can be a great way to practice!

4. It can be fun to play together as a family.

5. Mini-recitals in your living room can be used to push students to reach small goals.

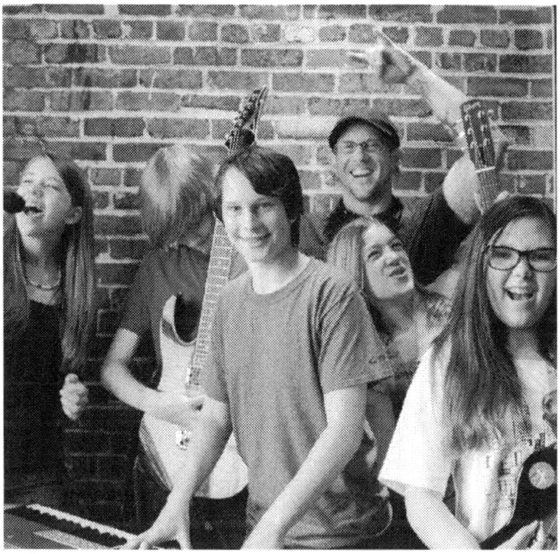

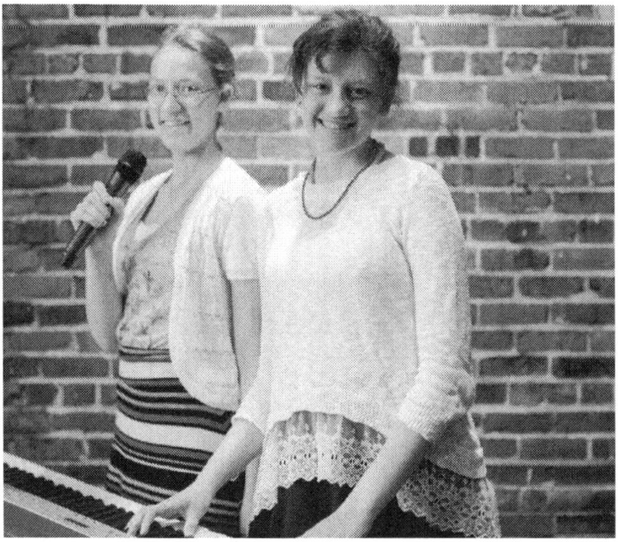

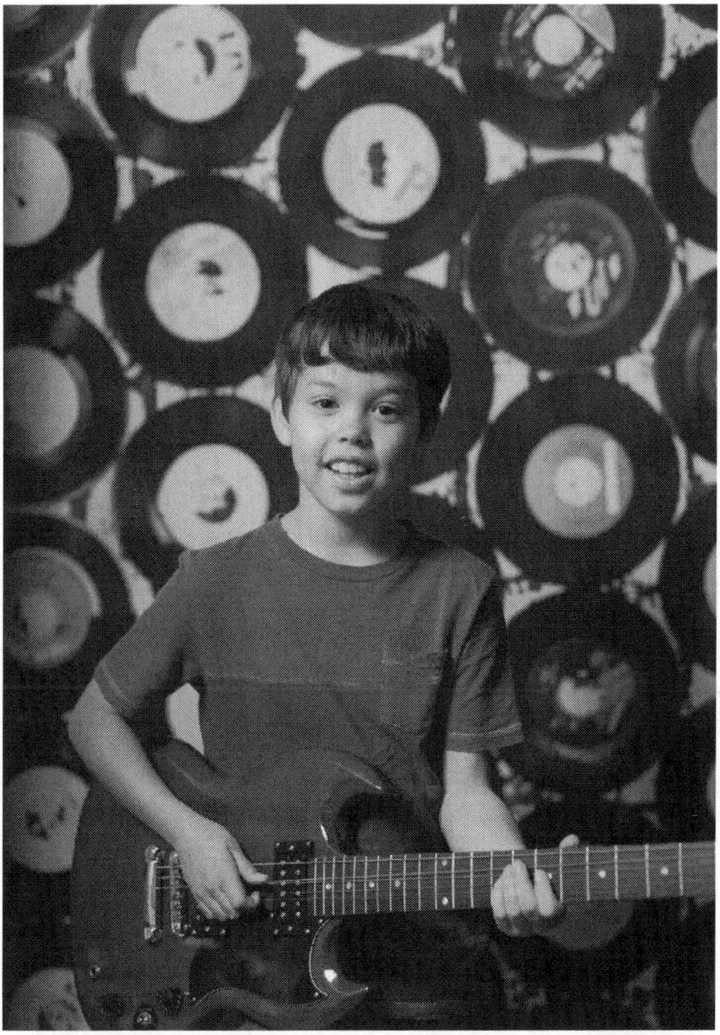

Chapter 8

10 Practicing Tips

1. Practice every day

It's very important to maintain a consistent practicing routine. Everyone has unavoidable conflicts, so it's okay to skip a day or two here and there. But if this happens, try to catch up with two practice sessions the day after.

When you practice with your instrument daily, it becomes a larger and more integral part of your life.

Consistency helps you retain what you have learned, and it helps you to see your progress.

Research has found that when you do something all the time, you will even dream about it when you sleep. That means your brain will actually continue to improve your abilities while you're sleeping!

2. When starting, practice for about 10 to 15 minutes each day.

Do not over-practice and turn it into a chore.

Keep your practice sessions light and simple.

This will help you retain a more positive attitude about practicing.

The key is to do this every day, and make it a part of your regular routine. We don't think twice about brushing our teeth every night, and it can be the same for practicing!

After a while, you will become ready to practice more, because you will really **want** to practice more.

3. Leave your instrument out where you can see it.

If you have an instrument that goes in a case, take it out of the case once you get home from your lesson.

Put it in a prominent, noticeable place.

Having it in plain sight will remind you to practice each day.

This will also show you that music is a part of your life, and that you are becoming a real musician!

Plus, if you have friends over, they will probably think it's pretty cool that you have an instrument. And guess what? It IS cool!

Singers should leave out books and CDs with backing tracks and sing in their bedroom, car, and family room.

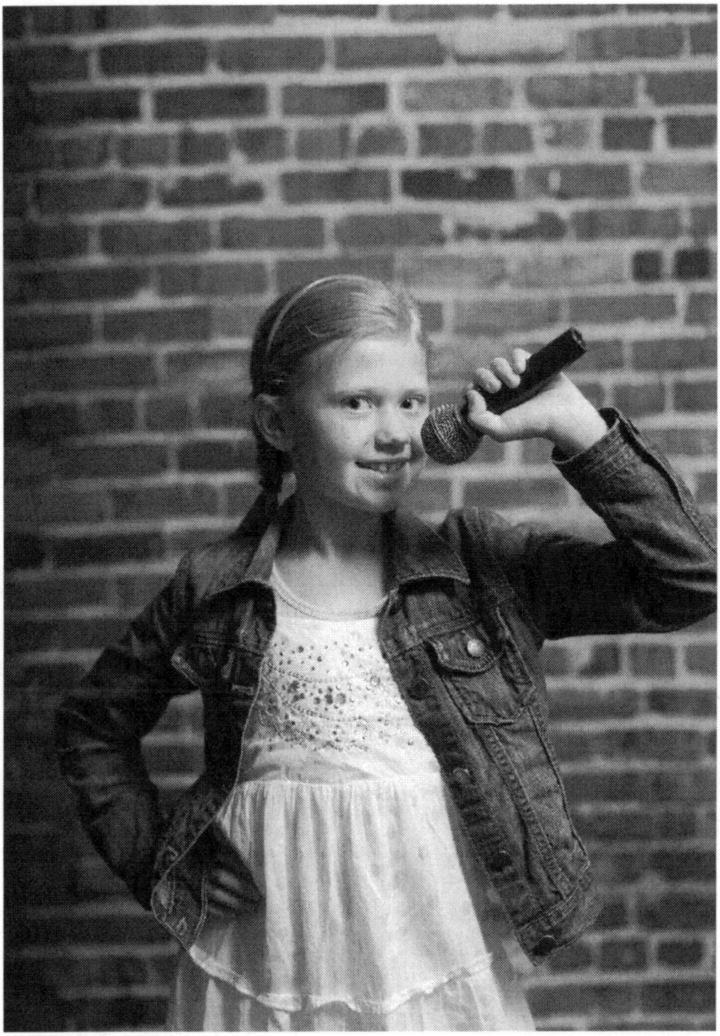

4. Put posters or pictures of your favorite musicians up in your practice area.

It doesn't matter if you practice in your bedroom, basement, or another area of your house or apartment. You should consider decorating at least part of it, to make it feel more like your designated practicing area.

When you do this, similar to leaving your instrument out, you reinforce the fact that you are a musician. It can really shift your mindset!

You can also find clocks, lamps, and many other items that are shaped like your instrument.

Any kind of music-related imagery can work. You can even clip photos from old books and magazines. It's all about making it personal!

5. **Practice at the same time each day.**

   Find a time that you will consistently have free for *Practice Time*.

   Then, stick with that time every day.

   This way, it becomes a natural part of your daily routine.

   When practicing is ingrained into your regular schedule, it is hard to forget to do it!

   Also, visualization is helpful. When you think about that time of the day, form a picture of it in your mind, and get excited about it! Imagine your practice session as a big step toward becoming the musician of your dreams.

6. Your attitude will take you far!

When you are learning to play a musical instrument, some things will be fun right away and some things will be more difficult.

Keep in mind that it might take more time to master certain lessons.

Never assume that something being hard means you're doing badly.

Always remember that with some more practice, you will get it down.

If you put in the effort, nothing will stop you. You will be AWESOME!

Keep that attitude with you always.

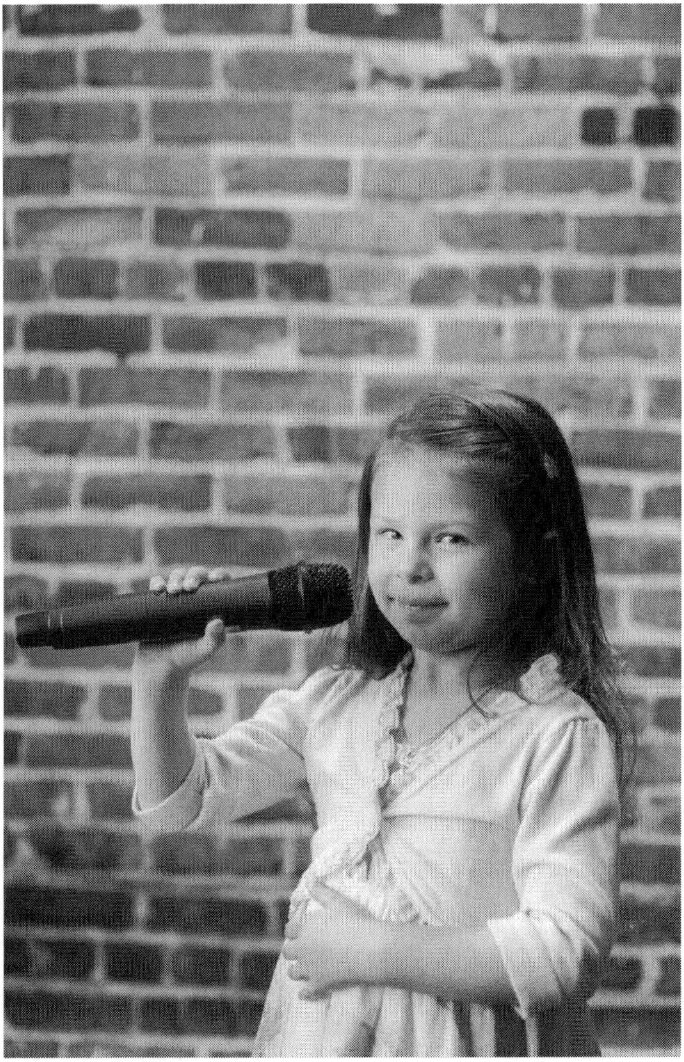

7. Parents need to tell their kids to practice.

Often, kids will not practice on their own. Actually, that's an understatement. Children will *almost never* practice without serious prompting.

Some of my advice here will help, but it's ultimately up to parents to get their kids to practice.

It's a great idea to make a weekly or monthly chart. Then, you can place little stickers on each day your children practice. Getting the chart filled with stickers is a great incentive.

Or take it one step further--once they attain a certain number of stickers, you can treat them to ice cream, a movie, museum, or whatever your kids love.

Once they've been practicing for a while, it will become habit, and your kids will start taking initiative on their own. Eventually they will thank you for pushing them!

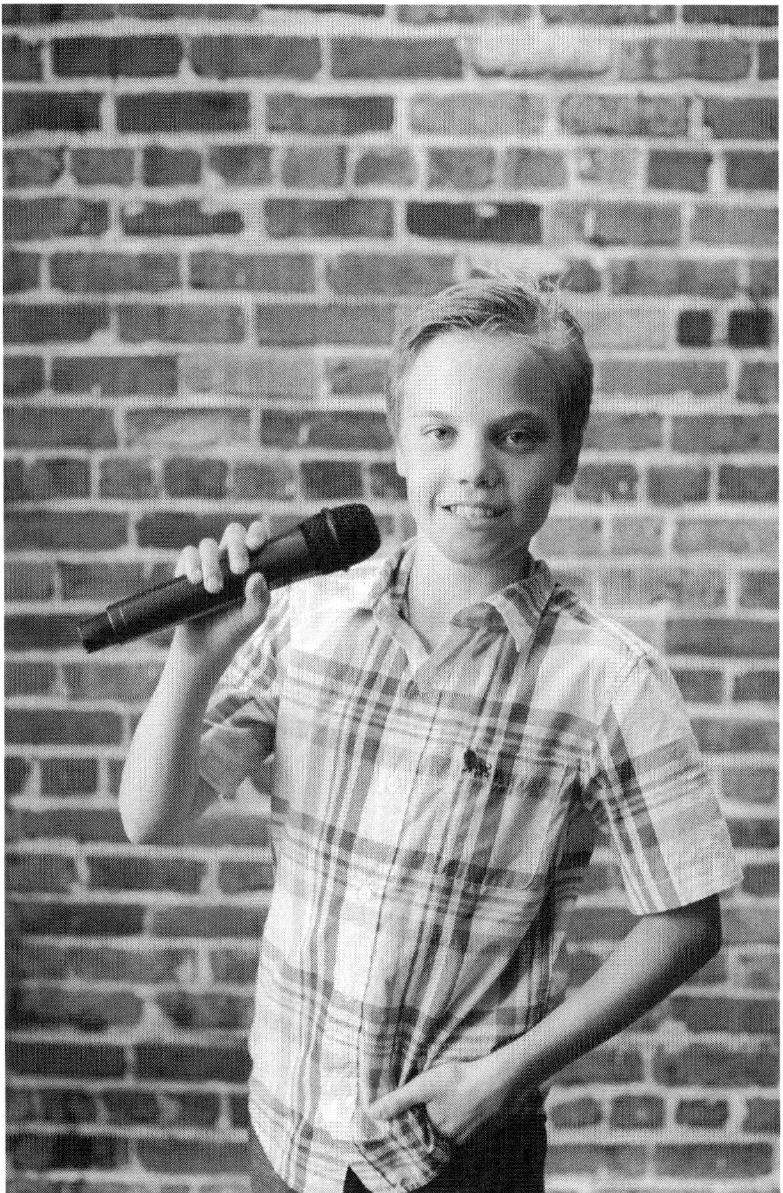

8. Practice slowly to master quickly.

When students are first starting out, most want to rush. It's great to be eager, but in this case, slow and steady definitely wins.

It's always important to practice very slowly when you are starting something new.

When practicing, do it as slowly as you need to be able to play it accurately, even if it is really, really slow.

If you go too fast for yourself, you will repeatedly make mistakes. Then, your subconscious starts to believe that you can't do it.

When you slow it down enough to succeed, your brain says, "Hey, I can do this!"

Once you perfect it at a slow pace, gradually work on getting faster. You will!

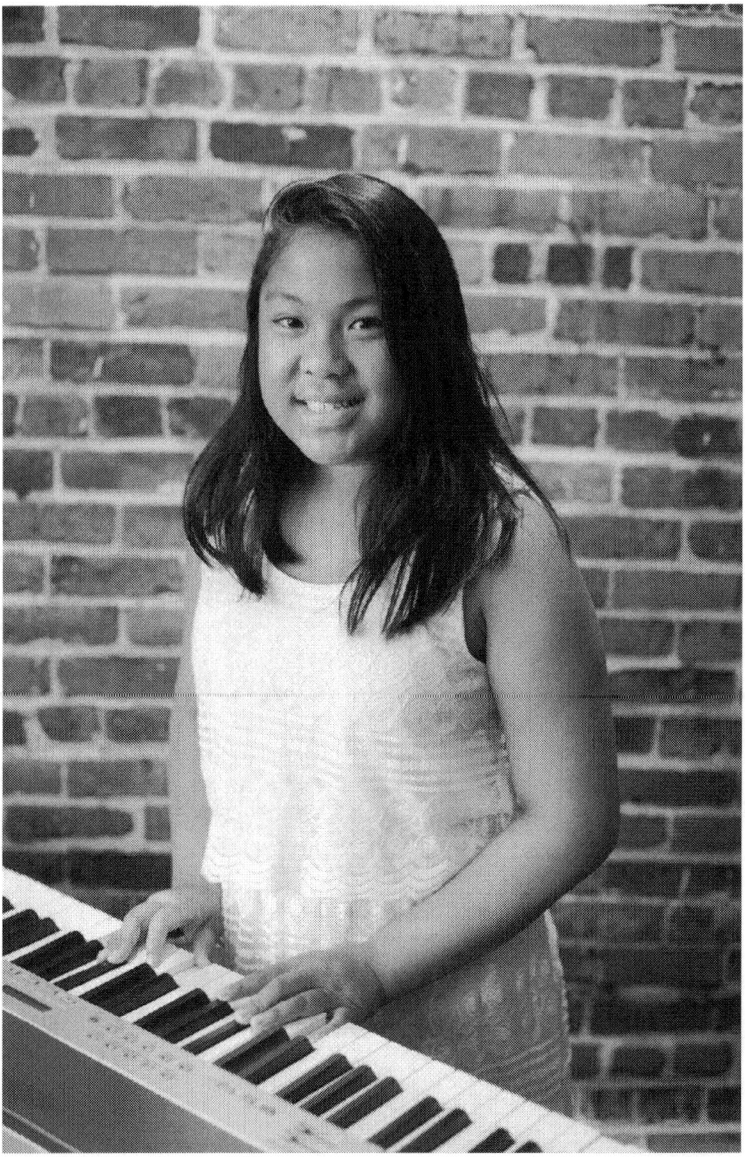

9. Watch other musicians and pretend you are them when you practice.

It's always helpful to look at someone who really knows how to play.

You can find clips on the internet, watch TV, a DVD, or see someone play live.

Observe what they are doing and how they look while they are playing.

Then, when you are playing a song or practicing, pretend you are that musician!

This technique, called modeling, can be very effective for learning and building confidence.

You can also use your teacher as someone to model.

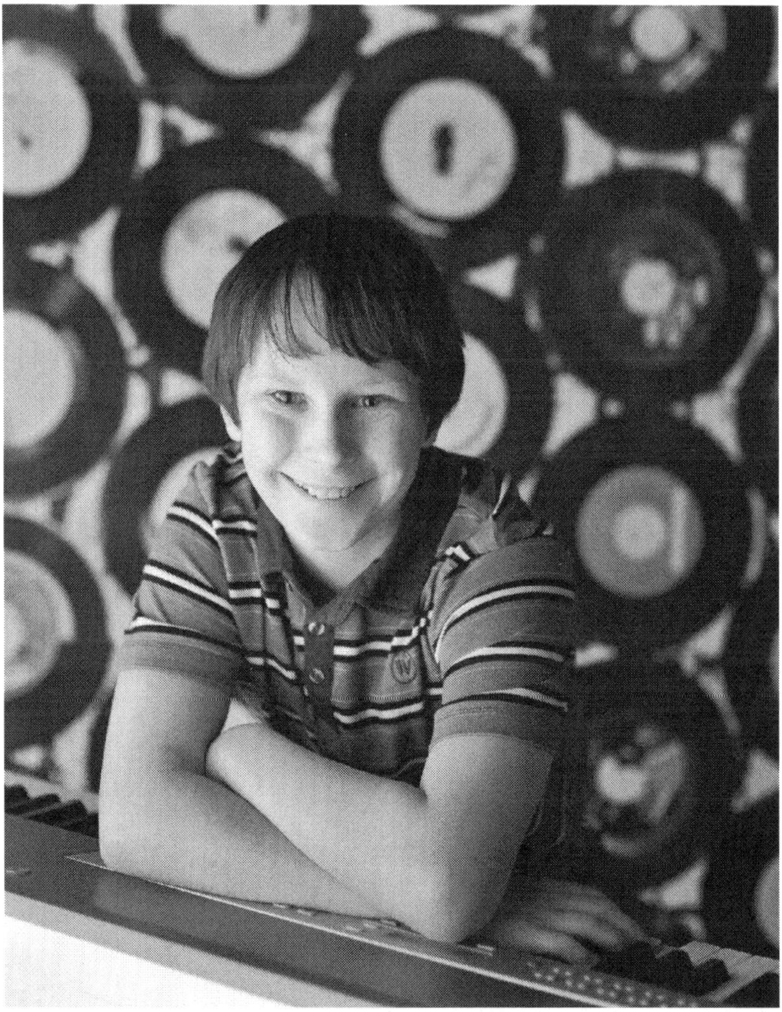

10. Set goals for what you want to learn and when you want to learn it by.

Having specific goals and deadlines will help increase your motivation levels.

When you are a new student, your teacher can help evaluate what goals will be attainable for you.

Later on, you will have the experience to judge for yourself what you can accomplish within a specific time period.

Think of it like a game. A fun challenge!

And if you picture it in these terms, you will want to WIN! What a great incentive!

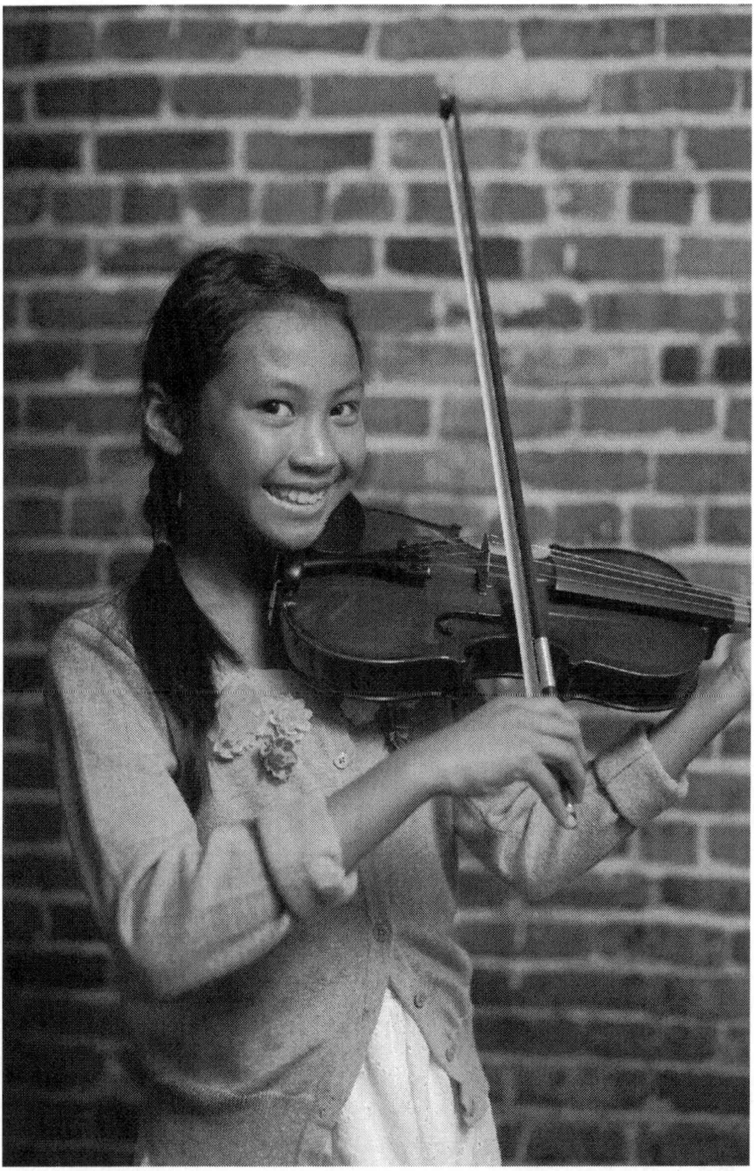

Chapter 9

Online Learning as a Great Supplement

We live in a world that is constantly changing and reinventing itself. Through technology and human ingenuity, we find new ways of doing things almost daily.

One of the new possibilities for students to learn music is taking advantage of online learning, such as YouTube videos, or music apps.

However, there is no doubt about the quality of your instructors when they are working in a real, brick and mortar building, versus teaching via the internet. Your teachers will have been hired by a trusted, highly-experienced music lessons authority, who has put them through the necessary background checks. There should also be an office staff that handles all the scheduling and billing.

There are many online lessons available that offer pre-recorded videos. These can get you started, but they are not tailored to you as an individual. You may end up learning from a specific method which isn't right for you. Plus, you can't ask questions or get advice specific to what you are practicing. Usually, the lack of communication involved with this method leads to frustration and alienation from the instrument.

There are also many websites that will connect you with teachers who have listed themselves as being available. Unfortunately, in these situations, there is no real screening process. It's difficult to tell if any of these teachers are right for you. They were never interviewed by someone with experience in what to look for in a teacher. Most often, they are teaching out of their living rooms without immediate access to the necessary tools for teaching.

Online learning is a great way to spark your interest and learning, and as a supplement between your lessons at your professionally-run music school, where the teachers have been hand-picked by a music lessons authority. You can find music online and bring it to your lesson. Then your teacher can communicate and tailor the lessons to your interests and skill level, getting you on the path to playing the music you love.

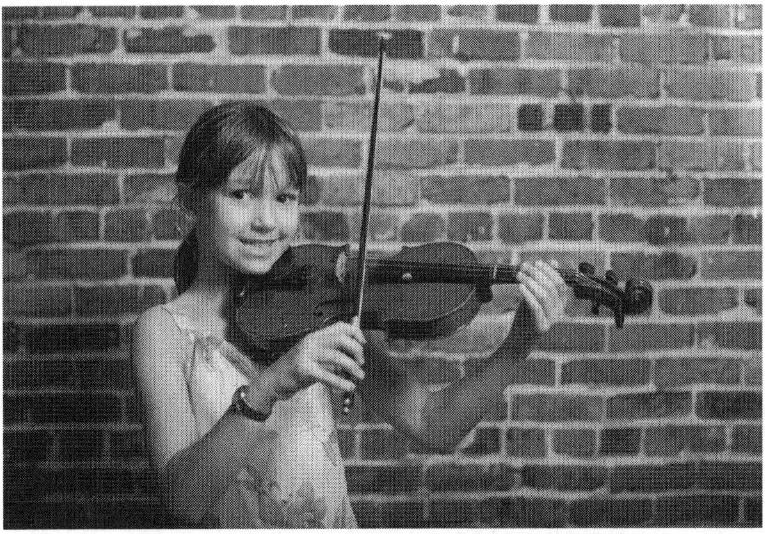

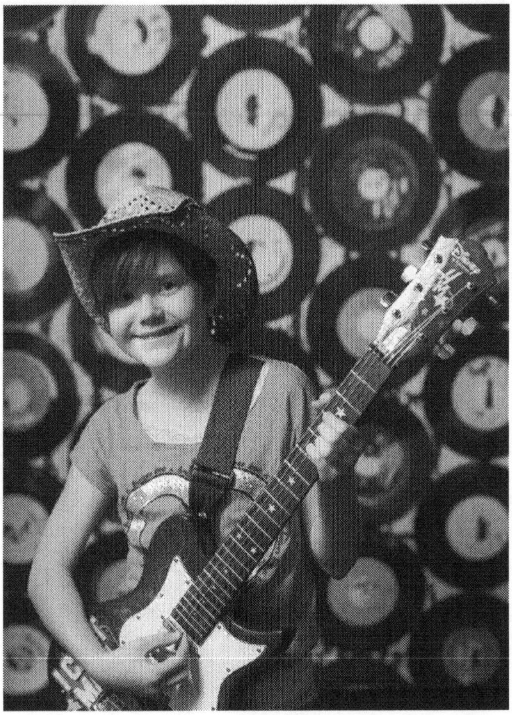

Chapter 10

Finding Your Place in Music

It's probably pretty obvious that I'm passionate about music and about private music lessons. Running a music school and writing a book are huge commitments.

I believe, based on both personal experience and what I've learned from others, that music lessons have something very special to offer a student.

It doesn't matter if you're doing it as a hobby, or if you have aspirations of becoming a professional musician. The benefits are numerous.

It has been a true pleasure and honor to have worked with thousands of students over my career. In teaching these students, I have learned so much.

I have learned how music can bring us all together, how it is universal, and can touch the hearts of people from all walks of life.

I have learned that we are all individuals, and that there are as many different ways to learn as there are people. There is no right or wrong way to learn. Talented teachers can work with students to find the methods that work best for each.

I have learned that music plants the seeds of optimism, and can help nurture happiness.

But my favorite thing is the opportunity I've had to learn a bit about each student's life. I've gotten to see how music has affected them in so many positive ways!

If you or a family member is thinking about starting music lessons, I highly encourage you to do so.

It has been the best thing I've ever gotten involved with, and I know you'll love it, too!

All of the principles and philosophies outlined in this book have been applied to my music academy in Rogers, Minnesota.

Rogers School of Music

www.rogersmusiclessons.com

Call (763) 670-8882 to talk with our friendly and helpful office staff and to get started with your music lessons!

Made in the USA
Middletown, DE
04 June 2017